LOOKING AFTER YOUR
Rabbit

Text by Clare Hibbert
Photography by Robert and Justine Pickett

Titles in the LOOKING AFTER YOUR PET series:

• Cat • Dog • Hamster • Rabbit
• Guinea Pig • Fish

© 2004 White-Thomson Publishing Ltd

Produced by White-Thomson Publishing Ltd
2/3 St Andrew's Place, Lewes, BN7 1UP

Editor: Elaine Fuoco-Lang
Inside design: Leishman Design
Cover design: Wayland
Photographs: Robert Pickett
Proofreader: Alison Cooper

Published in Great Britain in 2004 by Hodder
Wayland, an imprint of Hodder Children's Books.

This paperback edition published in 2007 by
Wayland, an imprint of Hachette Children's Books

Hachette Children's Books
338 Euston Road, London, NW1 3BH

The right of Clare Hibbert to be identified as the
author of this Work has been asserted by her in
accordance with the Copyright, Designs and
Patents Act 1988.

British Library Cataloguing in Publication Data
Hibbert, Clare
    Rabbit. - (Looking after your pet)
    1. Rabbits - Juvenile literature
    I.Title
    636.7'083

ISBN 978 0 7502 4524 1

Acknowledgements
The publishers would like to thank the following
for their assistance with this book:
With kind thanks for rabbits to Rosie Pilbeam
the Animal Care Unit, Canterbury College, Kent
and Herne Bay Pet Shop, Herne Bay, Kent.

Cover images: Photodisc/Getty Images

The website addresses (URLs) included in this
book were valid at the time of going to press.
However, because of the nature of the Internet,
it is possible that some addresses may have
changed, or sites may have changed or closed
down since publication. While the author,
packager and publisher regret any inconvenience
that this may cause readers, no responsibility for
any such changes can be accepted by either the
author, the packager or the publisher.

Printed in China

Contents

Keeping a rabbit 4

Choosing a rabbit 6

Your rabbit's home 8

Inside the hutch 10

Feeding your rabbit 12

Fresh foods 14

Together time 16

Playing outside 18

Rabbit habits 20

Cleaning out 22

Rabbit health 24

Holiday time 26

Rabbit facts 28

Glossary 30

Further Information 31

Index 32

Keeping a rabbit

The first question to ask yourself is "why do I want a rabbit?"

Rabbits are gentle and friendly. They make great pets. But before you decide a rabbit is the pet for you, check that you are ready to look after one. You will have to buy your rabbit a comfortable hutch, and a run for the garden.

▶ Rabbits are soft to stroke. They make adorable, cuddly pets.

Rabbits can live from six to twelve years on average and you will need to feed and play with your pet every day. You will also need to clean out its hutch, and find someone to care for your pet when you go on holiday.

Pet Talk

How many rabbits?

You can keep one rabbit, but it might get lonely. If you keep one rabbit you must give it as much attention as possible. It is better to keep two. So long as you have your pets neutered (see page 25), it does not matter whether you keep two bucks (male rabbits), two does (female rabbits) or one of each.

▲ If you have a pet guinea pig, you can let it graze in the run with your rabbit, but make sure you supervise the animals together. Provide each animal with its own hutch.

► This rabbit is a Lop. See how its ears hang down.

Choosing a rabbit

Look for a healthy baby rabbit.

▼ Don't be tempted to choose a rabbit you feel sorry for. Go for the liveliest of the litter.

Perhaps you know someone who has baby rabbits that need good homes. If not, try a pet shop, breeder or animal shelter. Baby rabbits are called kittens. They can leave their mothers when they are around seven to nine weeks old.

Choose the boldest kitten and ask to handle it. Then you can check on its health. Ask how big your rabbit will grow. Larger types might be too big for you to handle. Find out if your new pet is a buck or a doe.

Remember to find out what food your rabbit likes eating. Ask for a little of its bedding to put in its new hutch.

▲ When you take your new pet home, put it into its hutch straight away. Leave it alone for a few hours to get used to its new surroundings.

Top Tips

Choose a rabbit that has:

- smooth, glossy fur with no bare patches.
- bright, clear eyes and clean ears.
- clean, twitching nose – a sign that it is curious and playful.
- neat teeth that fit together.
- no overgrown claws.

▶ This rabbit looks healthy and alert. It will make a great pet if you look after it well.

Your rabbit's home

Prepare the hutch before you collect your new pet.

For one medium-sized rabbit, the hutch should be at least 150 cm long, 60 cm wide and 60 cm high. Buy a bigger hutch for two rabbits or one large rabbit.

The hutch should have a daytime area with a large wire-mesh door that lets in light and air. It will also need a connecting dark, cosy sleeping area with a solid, wooden door. Check both doors close securely. It should have a sloped overhanging roof covered in felt to help keep it waterproof. Put the hutch somewhere shaded from the sun and sheltered from the wind. The hutch should be raised off the ground to keep out damp.

▲ Building your rabbit a hutch can be fun, but make sure the hutch is properly weatherproof. A sloping roof will allow rainwater to run off.

Top Tips

Weather beaters

- In heavy rain, cover the hutch with heavy plastic.

- In freezing weather, move the hutch into a shed. Do not move it into a garage used by cars, though. Petrol fumes can kill rabbits.

- Do not put the hutch in a greenhouse – it will be too hot.

All rabbits will need a cosy home to live in. If you buy a hutch make sure it is the right size for your rabbit.

Put your rabbit's hutch in a sheltered spot, out of direct sunlight.

Inside the hutch

Make the hutch into a cosy home.

Line the hutch with newspaper and wood shavings. Do not use sawdust, which can damage your pet's breathing. Fill the sleeping area with hay. Fix a water bottle to the mesh door. You should also fix on a hay rack, to hold clean hay for your rabbit to eat. Put the food dishes in the daytime area. Add a piece of wood for your rabbit to gnaw on – this will stop its teeth getting too long.

▼ Get your rabbit's hutch ready before you bring your new pet home. Use the checklist to make sure you haven't forgotten anything.

Checklist: hutch kit

- Plastic drip-feed water bottle

- Two pottery food bowls – one for dried and one for fresh food

- Hay bedding

- Newspaper

- Wood shavings

- Fruit-tree branch or gnawing block

- Litter tray (see page 21)

▼ Use hay, not straw, for your rabbit's sleeping area. Straw stalks might hurt your pet's eyes.

Feeding your rabbit

Your rabbit needs regular meals.

Wild rabbits eat seeds, roots and grasses. You can feed your pet special rabbit food, which is a mix of dried cereal, seeds and rabbit pellets. Eating dry food is thirsty work, so keep your pet's water bottle topped up. You should also give fresh fruit and vegetables to your rabbit (see page 14).

▼ The water bottle should always have clean water for your pet to drink. Fill it with fresh water every day.

Feed your rabbit every morning. As well as the food mix, give your rabbit hay in a special hay rack. Fix the rack on the inside of the door, so the hay does not get wet when it rains.

▶ Make sure there is always fresh, sweet hay for your rabbit. Hay is very good for its teeth.

Top Tips

Feeding kit

🐾 Put your rabbit's food in a heavy, pottery dish that it cannot knock over.

🐾 Do not put a plastic food bowl in the hutch. Your rabbit will gnaw it and the sharp edges might hurt it.

🐾 Use a drip-feed water bottle rather than a water bowl, which might spill.

▽ If you feed your pet rabbit food, always provide hay, too. Most vets believe it is better for rabbits to eat only grass and hay.

Fresh foods

Your rabbit loves its greens!

Treat your rabbit to some fresh food every evening. About a handful is enough – too much will give your rabbit tummy ache. Always wash fresh food first.

Give raw root vegetables, such as carrots, parsnips and turnips. Once your rabbit is over 12 weeks old, you can also give greens including spinach and sprouts. Try peas, cauliflower, celery and parsley, too, but not lettuce as it can give your rabbit a stomach upset.

▶ Many fruits and vegetables are good for your pet – but only in small amounts. Take care not to give too many fresh treats.

As a treat, give your rabbit a slice of apple or pear, or even a strawberry. You will soon learn what your rabbit likes best.

Never leave uneaten fresh food in the hutch for more than a day, or it will go off.

Checklist: wild plants

Check wild foods with an adult. Your rabbit can eat:

- Chickweed
- Clover
- Dandelions

- Groundsel
- Shepherd's purse
- Yarrow

But these plants are poisonous:

- Anemone
- Buttercups
- Deadly nightshade
- Flowering bulbs
- Foxgloves

- Lily of the valley
- Poppies
- Privet

▼ This rabbit is enjoying a nibble of parsley. Use the checklist to make sure you do not feed your rabbit any poisonous plants.

Together time

Handle your rabbit every day to keep it tame and friendly.

For the first couple of days, just talk to your pet, so that it gets used to your voice.

Then you can begin to stroke and handle your rabbit. Scoop both hands under your pet's body and lift. Hold the rabbit close to your chest so that it feels safe and does not wriggle.

▶ As long as it feels safe, your rabbit will enjoy being cuddled and petted.

If your rabbit is long-haired, you will need to brush its coat every day. Short-haired rabbits like being groomed, too. Use an old, soft hairbrush – one that is only ever used for brushing your rabbit. Never try to give your rabbit a bath.

◄ Brush your rabbit with light, firm strokes. Always brush away from the head, towards the tail.

▼ The more you handle your rabbit, the tamer it will become. Find out where it likes to be tickled – but be gentle.

Top Tips

Rabbit handling

🐾 Do not disturb your rabbit if it is sleeping.

🐾 Never try to pick up your rabbit only by the scruff of its neck, or by the ears.

🐾 Be gentle! Never shout at or smack your rabbit.

🐾 Always put your rabbit back into its hutch bottom-first, so it cannot kick you.

Playing outside

Like you, your rabbit needs exercise.

In the wild, rabbits are free to run around. Your pet needs to stretch its legs too. Your rabbit will enjoy being in a run. Most runs are triangular-shaped and made of wire mesh. There should be a shaded section at one end where your rabbit can rest. Move the run around the lawn to give your rabbit fresh grass to nibble. Remember to fix·your rabbit's water bottle to the side of the run.

▼ Your rabbit can graze on fresh grass if you buy an ark like this one.

On fine days, you can put your pet in a run called a grazing ark. But never put the ark on grass that has been treated with weedkiller.

▼ This lucky pet has its own rabbit playground! If you have the space, ask an adult to help you build one. Your pet will have space to run around in safety.

Pet Talk

Rabbit playground

If you have space, make a rabbit playground. Put a 2-m-high fence around your rabbit's hutch. This must be sunk about 30 cm into the ground, so that your rabbit cannot burrow out. Cover the top with mesh too, to keep out cats, and place a ramp up to the hutch.

► Being outside on a sunny day is very good for your pet – so long as it has somewhere shady to rest. Sunshine helps the rabbit to stay healthy.

Rabbit habits

Your rabbit rubs its head against you to be friendly.

Some rabbits lick their owners, too! If your rabbit kicks or bites, say 'No' in a firm voice, then put it back in its hutch. It will soon learn not to be naughty.

Practise training your rabbit outdoors. You can also let your rabbit explore in the house. Make sure there are no electric cables around for it to chew. Some people keep their pet rabbit in the house all the time. House rabbits need a lot of attention and training.

► You can train your rabbit to come when you hold out some food. You can do this in the garden, but first make sure there is no way your rabbit can escape.

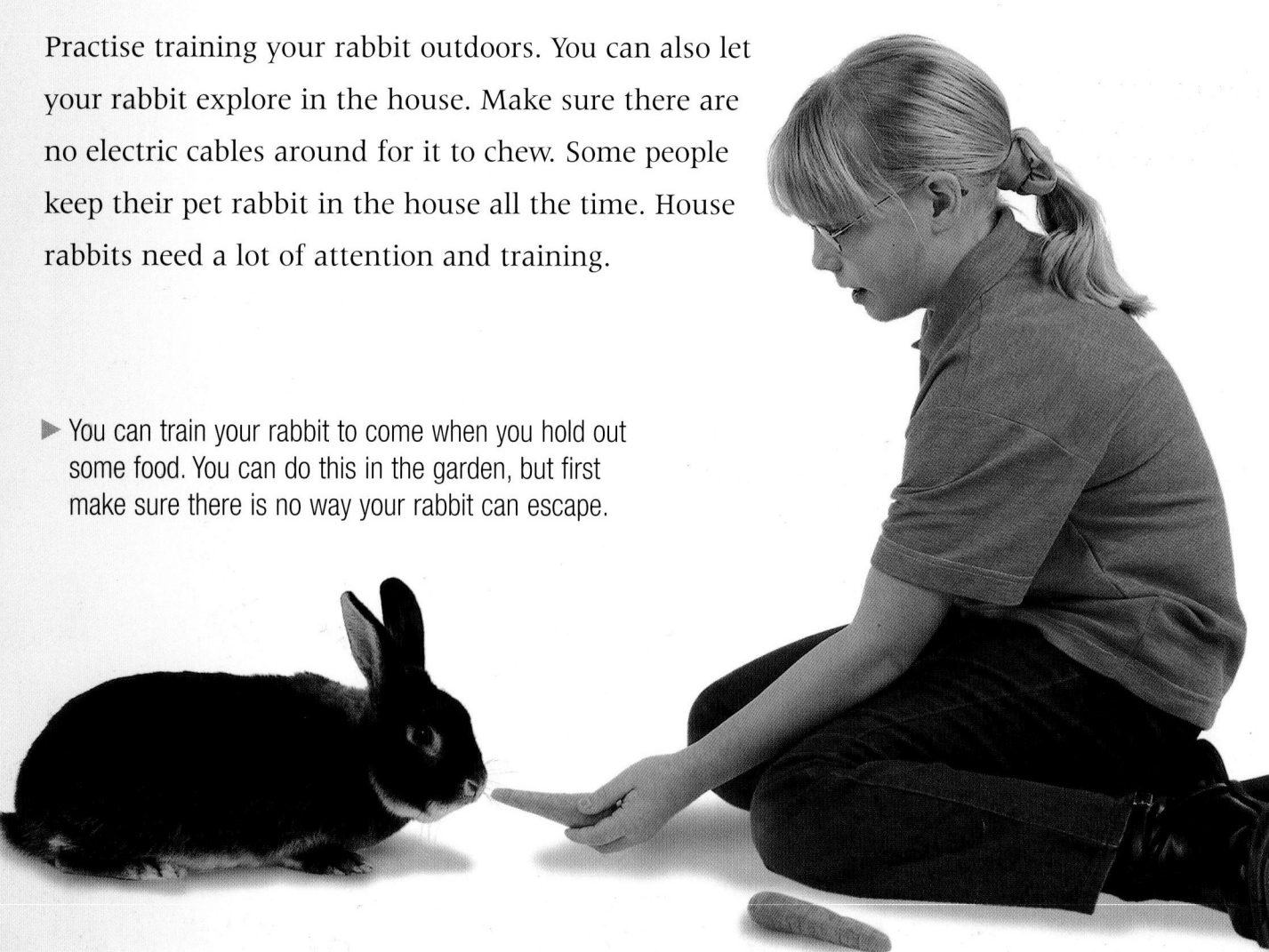

Pet Talk

Toilet training

House rabbits are toilet trained.
Outside rabbits can learn to use
a mini litter tray, too – and it
helps with cleaning out.
Add some soiled shavings
to show your pet what
the litter tray is for.

▲ House rabbits must be trained to use a litter tray.
Never use a plastic one, which your pet could chew.
A tin or enamel roasting dish would be ideal.

▼ Your pet can play indoors. Keep any doors
shut and do not let your rabbit climb stairs.
Keep it away from houseplants, too.

Cleaning out

Do not let your pet's hutch get dirty.

Check the hutch every day and take out any leftover food. Remove your rabbit's droppings and any wet bedding. Wash the food bowls and water bottle in warm, soapy water and rinse well. Clean the hutch thoroughly once a week. Put your rabbit somewhere safe, like its exercise run. Clear away all the old bedding, wood shavings and newspaper. Brush or scrape the dirt from the floor.

▶ Use a bottle brush to give the water bottle a thorough clean. Rinse well before you refill with clean water.

Now put down fresh newspaper and wood shavings. Fill the nesting area with clean hay. Every month or so, scrub the hutch with a special pet disinfectant. Rinse away all trace of disinfectant. Wait for the hutch to dry out completely before you put in the clean bedding.

▲ It is a good idea to wear rubber gloves when cleaning out your rabbit's hutch. A scrubbing brush should get rid of any caked-on dirt.

Checklist: cleaning kit

Keep all your cleaning equipment together and only use for cleaning out your rabbit.

- Rubber gloves
- Washing-up liquid
- Bottle brush
- Sponge
- Dustpan and brush
- Scraper
- Scrubbing brush
- Plastic bowl or bucket for hot water
- Special pet disinfectant
- Teatowel or paper towels

Rabbit health

Even healthy rabbits need to visit the vet once a year.

The vet will check your pet's health and give jabs to prevent serious diseases, such as myxomatosis. He or she will help treat fleas and also clip your rabbit's claws or teeth if they are too long. Never try to do this yourself.

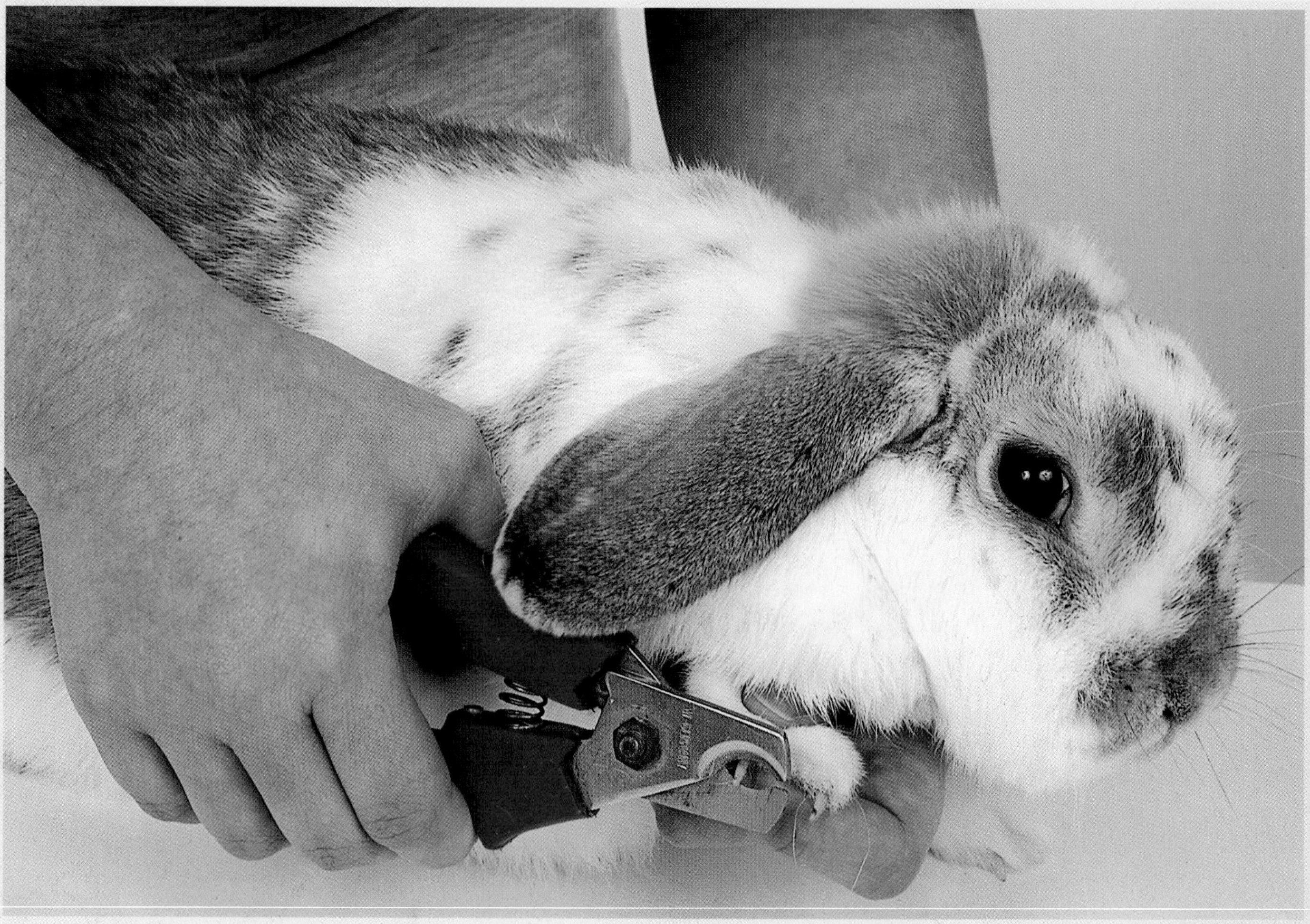

▲ Rabbits' claws never stop growing. If they become too long, take your pet to the vet to have its claws clipped.

▼ Baby rabbits are cute, but it is not a good idea to let your pet have babies. Ask your vet about neutering.

You will also need to visit your vet to have your pet neutered. Talk to your vet about this when your rabbit has its first check-up. Neutering stops female rabbits from having babies and can cut down on bad behaviour, such as fighting, in male rabbits. It is best not to breed rabbits – there are already so many unwanted pets that need homes.

Checklist: illness

If you see any of these signs of illness, take your rabbit to the vet:

- Dull fur
- Sores on its skin
- Dirty ears
- Runny eyes
- Sneezing
- No appetite
- Diarrhoea (upset tummy)
- Worms in its droppings
- Bloated tummy
- Not being very active

▼ You should check your pet's skin and fur each day, while you are handling it. The fur should gleam and the skin should be smooth.

Holiday time

When you go on holiday, do not forget your pet.

Ask someone to come and feed your pet twice a day and fill up the hay and water. It might be easier to take the hutch, food and equipment to your friend's house.

Write a list of what to do. Add your vet's telephone number in case your rabbit is ill. Spend time showing your friend how to handle your pet. Then your rabbit will not be frightened when you are away.

If you cannot find anyone to care for your rabbit, ask your vet for advice.

▼ Show your friend how to pick up and handle your rabbit.

Pet Talk

Meeting other animals

If your friend has rabbits, it is probably better to keep them apart from yours. Rabbits do not get on with cats or dogs either. If your friend has one of these, make sure they will be able to keep them away from your pet.

▲ Your pet might fight with your friend's rabbit. Make sure they are kept apart, even when they are grazing in the garden.

▶ Your rabbit will soon settle in if you give it some of its favourite food.

27

Rabbit facts

Bet you didn't know that the ancient Romans first brought rabbits to Britain! Read on for more fantastic facts.

- Rabbits' teeth never stop growing.

- The two most common wild rabbits are European rabbits and American cottontails. All pet rabbits are tame types of European.

- Wild rabbits live underground in warrens.

- Hares are related to rabbits, but they have longer ears and legs.

- A group of rabbits is called a herd.

- There are more than 50 different breeds of pet rabbit. The most popular is the Dutch.

- Rex rabbits are special breeds that have soft and velvety coats.

- Hair from Angora rabbits is spun into wool. In one year, you could collect about 500 g from one rabbit – enough for a very soft, fluffy jumper!

- The rabbit breed with the longest ears is the English Lop. One male, measured in 1996, had ears that were 75 cm long!

- Two New Zealand rabbits share the record for the largest litter. Both had 24 kittens.

- The largest rabbit breed is the White Flemish Giant. It can weigh up to 8 kg – about the same as a toddler!

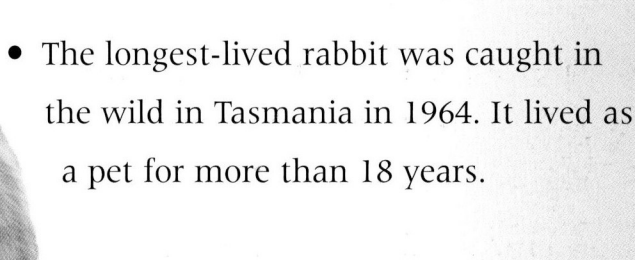

- The longest-lived rabbit was caught in the wild in Tasmania in 1964. It lived as a pet for more than 18 years.

Glossary

Animal shelter
A place that looks after lost or abandoned animals.

Breed
A particular type of rabbit, such as a Dutch, a Dwarf or an English Lop.

Breeder
Someone who keeps rabbits to mate them and produce babies to sell. He or she will want to produce kittens of a particular breed or type.

Buck
A male rabbit.

Disinfectant
A cleaning fluid that kills germs. Ask your vet or pet shop for a mild disinfectant that is suitable for cleaning your rabbit's hutch. Follow the instructions with care.

Doe
A female rabbit.

Fleas
Insect pests that sometimes live on rabbits. Ask your vet for advice on how to get rid of fleas.

Grazing ark
A triangular run, made of wire mesh, that you can put your rabbit in while it grazes on your lawn. The ark should have a a shaded area at one end.

Grooming
Cleaning a rabbit's fur. Short-haired rabbits can groom themselves, but long-haired ones need you to help by brushing them or they will get hairballs. (Pellets of hair that can clog up a rabbit's throat).

Jabs
Injections that protect against serious disease.

Kitten
A baby rabbit.

Litter tray
A shallow container where an animal can go to the toilet. If you have a house rabbit, you can train it to use a large litter tray. A roasting dish of enamel or tin is ideal. Never give your rabbit a plastic litter tray.

Myxomatosis
A disease that kills rabbits and is extremely catching.

Neutering
Removing a rabbit's sex organs. This stops females from getting pregnant and makes males less likely to get into fights.

Vet
An animal doctor.

Further information

Books

Looking After My Pet Rabbit by David Alderton
(Lorenz Books, 2002)

All About My Rabbit and Me by Don Harper
(Hamlyn Young Books, 1999)

My Pets: Rabbit by Honor Head, photographs by Jane Burton
(Belitha, 2003)

Looking After Your Rabbit by Helen Piers
(Frances Lincoln, 2002)

My First Rabbit by Veronica Ross
(Belitha, 2004)

Useful addresses

PDSA
Whitechapel Way
Priorslee
Telford
Shropshire
TF2 9PQ
Tel: 01952 290999
Fax: 01952 291035
Website: www.pdsa.org.uk

RSPCA
Wilberforce Way
Southwater
Horsham
West Sussex
RH13 9RS
Tel: 0870 3335 999
Fax: 0870 7530 284
Website: www.rspca.org.uk

Index

b

baby rabbits (kittens) 6, 25, 29
bedding 7, 10, 11
breeds 5, 28, 29
bucks 5, 6

d

does 5, 6

e

exercise 18, 19

f

food and drink 7, 10, 12, 13, 14, 15, 18
foods to avoid 14, 15

g

gnawing blocks 10, 11
grazing arks 19
grooming 17

h

handling 6, 16, 17, 26
hay 10, 11, 13, 23
health 6, 7, 24, 25
house rabbits 20, 21

hutches 4, 5, 7, 19
cleaning a hutch 22, 23
preparing a hutch 8, 9, 10, 11

j

jabs 24

k

kittens 6, 25, 29

l

litter trays 11, 21

n

neutering 5, 25

p

poisonous plants 15

r

runs 4, 5, 18, 19

t

teeth 7, 10, 24, 28
toilet training 21
training 20, 21

v

vets 24, 25, 26

w

water bottles 10, 11, 12, 13, 18, 22